It's intriguing. I couldn't put it down. I had to read it to the end.'
Stefan – Owner, Eurostat Group

'It made me want to pick it up and read it again. In fact, I'm going to do just that tonight.'
Ashley – MD, LA Design

'It made me smile. It made me laugh. I couldn't put it down.' **Conny**

'This book has helped me write that letter, make that phone call.' **Adrian**

'I find your book so exciting and so wonderfully helpful. I have read it again and again and each time find deeper wisdom, a pearl of great price, or a light shining out of a particular sentence or phrase.' **Marie**

THE A - Z OF POSITIVE THINKING

'There is no doubt your book is food for thought for the hungry – fulfilling a great need.' **Constance**

'Enlightened people lead us back into truth... I believe you are such... you truly must go on with your work. You are a lighthouse in a storm-tossed sea.' **Megan**

'I thank you for your book. It enabled me to give a push to a boulder on my own road. Now I can go a little further along the path.' **Annie**

'I thought it a pity some of the best passages were right at the end – hidden away. But where else could they be? A true student/seeker will go right to the end and find them.' **Maja**

THE A-Z OF POSITIVE THINKING
THE **PRESS**

'The A-Z of Positive Thinking is definitely a good idea… It tells us that there are three times as many negative words as positive ones. The important ones – the positives – are listed and are called 'antidotes to negativity'. This book is a good introduction to positive thinking.'
Women's Health Magazine

'Examples of how to think positively and banish negative feelings. Putting the positive words together will make you giggle. The overall effect of the book is uplifting.'
Daily Mail – Book of the Week

'A call to accentuate the positive… Excuses and negative thinking are diseases that can blight your life according to this book that promotes positive words as the antidote. Positive words are the essential medicine, the cure, to give you the power of positive thought.' Farmers Weekly – Editor's Choice

THE A - Z OF POSITIVE THINKING

READERS QUOTES

'Very clever and well written.'
- **Jean McCulloch**

'I stopped in the middle of writing a speech. I was frustrated, anxious, lost for ideas – until I dipped into your book. It got me back on track. It's Excellent, Accomplished, Fulfilling, Happy, Invaluable, Invigorating, Masterful, Powerful, Profound and Therapeutic. Thanks – **Carpe Diem.**' – **Ian MD, Reliance Group**

'It is a truth that personal fulfilment is linked to the degree of control people feel they have over their own lives. This book helps people gain that control.'
Nic MD, Serial Entrepreneur

'It made me laugh.'
Linda MD, Packaging Team

'I know you will rejoice in the transformation your book brought about in the daughter of a friend of mine. "She was 40. Her marriage was on the rocks. Her children were neglected. She had a wretched job. She was overweight, ungroomed and uncouth.

She popped into see me last Friday. Had her son not been with her I would not have recognised her. She was full of light, beautiful, well-groomed, and happy. She has a wonderful new job and is considered the best. She is interested in and caring for her children. She has lost loads of weight. She told me, "Two years ago you gave me a small yellow book. I read it three times and decided I would do what it said and have done so faithfully ever since. Every morning, on getting out of bed, I go to my bathroom mirror and tell myself – 'I am loving, beautiful and successful'. The results have been quite dramatic". A wonderful transformation Neil...' **Constance**

THE A - Z OF POSITIVE THINKING

'I began to read your 'A-Z' in the bath and did not realise until I got to the end that my bath was cold, the bubbles had dissolved, and I looked like a prune! I was so captivated and empowered by this. What an incredible gift!' **Sarah**

'I found your book very inspiring. It will help me a lot in the future as I start my career as a hospital doctor. Thank you.' **Jan**

'After reading your book I have done three things. 1. Written an article based on Living, Laughing, Loving and Learning. 2. Helped lift my girlfriend out of a deep gloom. 3. Cheered up my grandma after her recent bereavement. Your book has a good effect on people.' **Will**

'I love the 'A-Z'. It was amazing how answers can appear from nowhere just by opening it on a random page. The happy, healthy, horny and holy combination is definitely a reframe on life!! – I am full of admiration.' **Liz**

'Your 'A-Z' was a joy to read. It is a perfect gift and a complete insight.' **Claire**

'Thank you: for writing your valuable, happy book. Smiling is important to me and your positive antidotes make me smile. Let's smile some more and make the world a happier place.' **Louise**

'This book is easy to read, flows well and has excellent, strong relevant content.' **Piera**

'I like this book very much and always have it by my side for regular reading.' **David**

THE **A - Z** OF POSITIVE THINKING

'This book is absolutely marvellous, and I refer to it often. Thank you for sharing your experiences.' **Gerry**

'This is a very fine book. It gave me great pleasure and I was very impressed. It helps restore the old 'Joie de vivre'. I believe this book will be a great success.' **Dave**

'Good book - Sensible stuff.' **Denise**

Amazon – Readers Feedback: 4.7 / 5 STARS

'Wonderful insight – this book changed my thoughts.' – **Marc**

'As human nature has it, we tend to tell ourselves what we cannot achieve instead of what we can. Neil's short but concise book turns around the negative thought process. Brilliant inspiration into life's wonders and what we make of them... all in words and how we use them. Recommended for those, who want to be reborn.' 4 STARS

'I bought this book for myself a long time ago and it has brought so much into my life even though it is only a small book. It is pure positive thinking in its very essence. You can have books that dilute it and waffle on but why? When here is the very book, you need. I am now on here to buy this book for my teenage daughter as mine, as so many of my best books, has been borrowed – never to be returned.' **Bojo** – 5 STARS

'I have bought a number of these little books for different people and like it very much.' **Molly** 5 STARS

THE A - Z OF POSITIVE THINKING

'If you are interested in the effects of your thoughts on your life, this is a fab book to carry around in your pocket, so that you can refer to it when you slip into negative thinking mode. If you change your vocabulary, you are in effect changing your mind. A good, zippy, to-the-point book.' **Shine** 5 STARS

'Love this book – One of the best.' **Sam** 5 STARS

'Positive words – I positively know it will help!' **Bas** 4 STARS

'Your book encapsulates your attitude to life. It has changed my life. I love it …!' **Caroline** 5 STARS

About the Author

Neil is a graduate in Marine Engineering and has sailed around the world as a ship's engineer. Somewhere on that voyage he discovered a passion for personal development. Landing in California he worked for Dale Carnegie before returning to the UK to build a business for them in South London. Being entrepreneurial he quickly set up his

THE **A - Z** OF POSITIVE THINKING

own coaching and consulting business. He has had the privilege of working with 6961 people in 257 businesses in the US, Europe, and the Middle East.

Neil loves creating innovative approaches to helping businesses develop individuals, teams and divisions resulting in the formation of Perfect Teams in 2016. Using a unique algorithm 'Perfect-Teams' has become the new standard for helping businesses to understand the mix of people they have in their teams.
www.perfectteams.co.uk

People often describe Neil as - Enigmatic, Quiet and Driven.

When not consulting or coaching you will find Neil running or trekking the Surrey Hills or similar vistas around the world.

Dedication

To Caroline with Love

THE **A - Z** OF POSITIVE THINKING

THE A-Z OF POSITIVE THINKING

A New Vocabulary to Change Your Life

NEIL JAMES TUSON

THE A - Z OF POSITIVE THINKING

Published by
Filament Publishing Ltd
14, Croydon Road, Beddington,
Croydon, Surrey CR0 4PA
+44(0(20 8688 2598
www.filamentpublishing.com

The A-Z of Positive Thinking
by Neil James Tuson
Cover Design - Rob Arnold
ISBN 978-1-913623-73-9

First published in Great Britain in 1994 as
'The A-Z of Thought Antidotes'

All rights reserved
No portion of this work may be copied in any
way without the prior written permission of
the publisher

Introduction 2022

What's changed in twenty-five years? Everything, and not a lot! The 'everything' includes the internet, smartphones, the world-wide-web, email, on-line shopping, social media, and for some of us, children. The 'Not a lot', the stark difference between a positive point of view and the negative. What else has changed? Hopefully our individual levels of learning, and the ability to cope with the accelerating pace of chane.

I know that my skill set has improved immeasurably over the years, and one key aspect is due to having a son and the lessons children can teach us adults. But before we get to that, let me start with a thousand bankers!

"The grand old Duke of York, he had ten thousand men, he marched them up to the top of the hill, and he marched them down again.

And when they're up they're up, and when they're down they're down, d when they're only halfway up, they're neither up nor down!"

"I had to smile as I watched and got a thousand bankers at a time to participate in the old nursery rhyme. They rose as one, they fell as one and they buzzed with energy and laughter as one. From Manchester to Birmingham to Brighton, it's the best fun I've ever had in a suit."

"But why?" you ask.

"Well, I'll tell you why shortly, but let me tell you about my son and how I got him to start managing his temper tantrums when he was about ten."

"We were getting a birthday card for his grandmother one Saturday. As we were walking to the post office, he starts to go off on one in the middle of the street. It was quite a scene I can assure you.

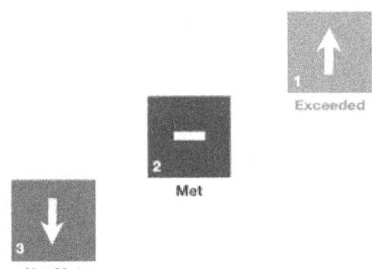

I let it go for a while and then took hold of his shoulders and started screaming back.

He's that shocked he immediately stops and starts laughing, telling me what a crazy dad he has.

'Yes, I am and I'm about to get crazier because I'm going to teach you the biggest lesson of your life in the next five minutes. James, fundamentally there are three kinds of people in the world - Happy people - Neutral people – Unhappy people. Just see them all as being inside three different boxes.

THE **A - Z** OF POSITIVE THINKING

Which of the three boxes would you have been sitting in?'

'Guess the unhappy box, dad,' he responded with a curious expression.'

'Right. So, look around you as we walk down the street and tell me which of the boxes people sit in as we go.'

'OK. That was fun,' he said as we arrived at the post office.

'What did you notice?' I asked him.

'Well unhappy people just seem to radiate this zone of gloom around them which you don't want to get close to, and happy people just give off a wave of attraction and I found myself drawn to them. The neutral people were just calm.'

'Good observation,' I replied. 'Now I need to draw this out for you to explain the lesson. I'll draw the boxes first from bottom left to top right and I'll number them 3, 2, and 1 see.

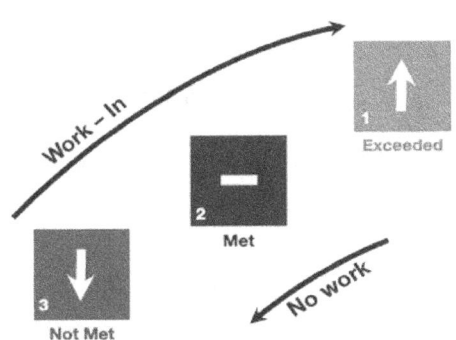

Now, people's happiness can be likened to their energy levels. When they're happy they're up, and when they're unhappy they're down. I'm going to represent that by three symbols. An up arrow, a down arrow, and a neutral sign, which is just a dash – just so. Now do you remember the last time you saw your grandfather?'

'Yes. He was a legend 'cos he gave me twenty pounds pocket money instead of ten.'

"How did that make you feel?'

THE A - Z OF POSITIVE THINKING

'Very happy indeed, I suspect you're going to tell me that that is an up-arrow event.'

'Quick thinking, I am indeed. Now the thing about energy is that it's always going to flow downwards over time. Hot things get cold. Rivers run downhill. Money gets spent. I'm going to put this up arrow in the top right-hand box 1. Now do you remember how you felt the week before when your grandfather gave you your usual tenner?'

'Yeah. I just felt OK about it. Guess I'd kind of got used to him always giving it to me as I left. I can see that that's going to be the neutral sign in box 2 and you don't have to ask me about box 3 because I can see that that's that time when he didn't give me anything.'

'Do you remember how you felt as we drove away?' I asked.

'I was really upset.' He replied.

'Do you remember why you were upset though?'

'Because I was meeting up with Dan and I was expecting to get the money that evening so that we had something to go out with and I had nothing, and it was just so unfair, and I bet he didn't treat my cousins that way!' he started to shout.

'OK stop now. Here's where the lesson really comes together. Box 3 is all about that negative energy and emotion. Most negativity is caused, by someone having an expectation that is not met or a promise not delivered, an expectation that is thwarted. The key thing to understand though, and if you get this, you'll be light years ahead of all the other kids you know and most of the adults too, the key thing is that ninety-five per cent of all that down energy is self-generated because someone had a fantasy about their expectations, or they made an assumption about something, or they took something for granted.

THE **A - Z** OF POSITIVE THINKING

In other words, there was never any conversation, or agreement, or clear rules and boundaries around things. Then when it didn't happen, they got themselves upset.'

'But dad,' he interrupted. 'If you don't get something you're going to be upset. I don't understand.'

'No James and neither do most of the human race. The big lesson is that you control your emotions and feelings. No one does it to you. You do it to you. It's your responsibility to control your own energy. When it does it to you, you are simply being a victim and then you're at the effect of things and you will live a box 3 life which is a woeful and sorrowful thing.'

'OK dad I think I get it but what do I do to stay out of box 3?'

'Well, the sane place to live is in box 2. This is where you cause things to happen. You become the architect of your own future.

This is where you have conversations with people about things. You draw up contracts and agreements. You get clear with people how things are going to be. You share with people what your thoughts and expectations are. Then if there's any disagreement you get to make choices on what to do. Those choices may mean you negotiate a compromise, or it may mean you decide to walk away. The fact is that it's a cleaner way of conducting things and it stabilizes the energy.'

'Seems like a lot of hard work to me.'

'And that James is exactly why most people end up living in box 3. It requires work and people want to go with the flow and have an easy life. The tragedy is it ends up not being an easy life. The easier life is the one in which someone takes responsibility and ends up making things happen for them. Now I just need to check in with you on how much of this you have understood. Here's the back of a paper bag and a pen. You teach me son.'

'Well dad, the way I see it there are these three different squares. In this one is a house where the roof is blown off, all the windows are smashed, and the door is hanging off.

There's also thunder, lightning and sheets of rain. People are huddling together and look pretty miserable. In this square the people have taken responsibility to look after the house and you can see them looking out the window all warm and cosy as the storm passes. And in square one there's brilliant sunshine, flowers are blooming, there's a dog, and a couple looking very happy indeed having a picnic on the lawn.'

'That's brilliant James, very good indeed. So, the next time you start like you did back in the street I'm simply going to name the behaviour and call you, box 3 boy, and ask you what you're going to do to change your attitude. OK?'

'Sure pops. You certainly are one crazy guy.'

And maybe I am. How many fathers have talks like that with their children? But what's the correlation with the Grand old Duke of York, and a thousand bankers, I hear you ask? It's all about that energy. Is it up, down, or only halfway? Where's your own?

At the time I was warming the conference hall up for a corporate briefing. I wanted to show that we control our own energy levels and attitudes but there was another reason too. The guy I was doing the tour with had bet me before the first show that I couldn't get one of the bankers up on stage to recite a nursery rhyme.

THE **A - Z** OF POSITIVE THINKING

I smiled as I took the bet and said to him, 'What's it worth if I get all of them to do it?'

"Bad habits are easy to come by, but hard to live with. Good habits are hard to come by, but easy to live with!" This book will help you to develop good habits.

Neil James Tuson
London

ORIGINAL PREFACE – 1994

This book like any project, started with a small seed of an idea. The eventual stimulus to write it all down and publish was a negative experience that, once antidoted and negated, turned into an outstanding opportunity for personal growth.

They say that even something as beautiful as a pearl starts as a small piece of grit inside the oyster. That's how I now see that initial stimulating event: another bit of grit in life from which to learn, grow and further the path of love and life.

I know from personal experience, business, and testimony from friends that all these strategies do work.

THE **A - Z** OF POSITIVE THINKING

As I say in my classes, if you like the ideas – great! Use them - work with them. If on the other hand, you don't see anything of value to you – great! Just trash the idea and move on to another that feels right for you. There are no right or wrong ways in growing. Growth happens because we want it to happen.

Neil James
London
November 1994

ACKNOWLEDGEMENTS

Arthur Koestler said in his book *The Act of Creation* that humour, much like creativity, comes from a sudden shift in our perception – a shift from one framework or perspective to another. In an instant a realisation reveals itself to us. Suddenly we see or think of everything differently.

I've always relished those slips, those sudden shifts in perspective. I say always, but that is not exactly true. Many of them I did not like at all at the time. Rather I grew to appreciate them, in much the same way as I now enjoy a mature-single-malt.

THE **A - Z** OF POSITIVE THINKING

Acknowledgements are my maturing appreciations. This book is a consequence of many slips and shifts, of failures turned into successes. It could not have occurred without others being involved, without slips and bridges between personalities. The inspiration comes from others; from ideas distilled, crystallised, internalised, reformulated, shifted and moved.

I wish to acknowledge the writings of James Kavanaugh and in particular his poem, 'Will You Be My Friend', which helped me on my path.

On this path I've received help, support, and encouragement from the following: Caroline Rogers, Charlie Tveit, Ashley Wallman, Ilesh and Dushyant Patel and the many people I've been fortunate enough to meet in my chosen profession.

Special tributes are owed to Tess Moore for her creative input, Isabel Losada my agent and Judith Longman my editor.

I am also deeply grateful to Teresa who in large measure was the catalyst and inspiration for bringing this book to print.

THE A - Z OF POSITIVE THINKING

THE SEED OF AN IDEA

Have you ever wondered where all the negativity comes from? Why it is, that with all that's great, good, and beautiful, that we still seem to naturally gravitate back to those good old negs?

Well, it might have a lot to do with the fact that in an average-sized dictionary containing 31,460 words, there are only 1,705 that can be seen to be positive, strong, powerful and stimulating. That is just over 5 per cent of the words available to use. Moreover, there are over three times as many disempowering, sniping, griping, belittling and critical negative words. With 5,890 negatives to 1,705 positives, is it any wonder that the natural flows of conversation, thought and ideas are going to be strongly biased to the negative, especially when we seem to be able to roll the negatives off our tongues at a rate far in excess of three to one!

We are essentially our thoughts, and our language is going to be dramatically influenced by those thoughts. So if I have any goal in mind at all for this book, it is to reverse the trend for negative thinking, language and actions and to make a difference to the ways in which we use our minds in any given set of circumstances, As George Bernard Shaw was so fond of quoting,

'I don't believe in circumstances, for the people who get on in this world are the people who go out and look for the circumstances they want and if they can't find them, they make them.'

So where did the idea for this book of positive words come from? What was the seed?

THE **A - Z** OF POSITIVE THINKING

I was at a conference in York. As I walked past a group of our Swiss associates, I overheard part of their conversation. "The secret is you have to be **Living, Laughing and Learning.**" That was it; that was all. Just a snippet of a conversation. About what I have no idea, but as I walked past, it captured a piece of my mind and stayed there working and growing. Now I'm a magpie for ideas. I carry a small red notebook with me at all times, to jot down thoughts, impressions, quotes and ideas, and this little snippet went straight inside. It did more than that though. It continued to work at me and I found myself playing with the concept. **Living, Laughing and Learning.** Powerful, positive, empowering words. Words of life.

When I returned from the conference, I wrote the three words up on the dry-wipe board I have in my office and let the idea stay in limbo for a while. Like any true idea, it didn't just stay still.

This one started to grow, slowly at first, with the addition of just one word – Loving. I felt this was a stronger message, that this is what life is all about – **Living–Laughing–Loving–Learning** – and I adopted it as my motto.

Over the period of a month or so, three other letters appeared on my office board, attracting for a number of reasons their own words which were:

*Fun–Free–Friends-Fame
Happy–Healthy–Horny–Holy
Energetic-Exciting-Enthusiastic-
Extraordinary*

I started trying them out. People would ask, "How are you?" and I'd say right back, "Well. I'm Happy, Healthy, Horny, and Holy". Some people would look at me as if I was totally crazy, but the majority would smile, and if I'd used the Es they would say, "You certainly are extraordinary!" The point though is that I was having fun with it and I noticed other people's attitudes and mine shifted as a consequence. It sure beat that old litany of 'Oh, I'm all right, how are you?' or that old faithful, 'Oh, not too bad today. My neck's playing up a bit. Pity it's so cold. How about you? Still got that trouble with your back?'

As with anything that works, you start to explore it a little more and so I started another notebook, indexed A-Z no less, and started jotting down all the good words I came across: Terrific, Exotic, Radiant, Enthralling, Sensational, Artistic, Alluring, Noble, Natural, Erotic, Tender, Unique, Real, Now, Enterprising, Remarkable, Inspiring, Spectacular, Beautiful and many more.

As the notebook slowly and gradually began to fill up, I started to notice a dramatic shift in my attitude to situations and people.

An additional benefit, which was to prove very useful later on, was that by simply reading or speaking aloud the positive words, I was able to change my state of mind, my attitude, remarkably quickly.

ATTITUDES

There are times when a thought strikes you and you go 'Aha!/Eureka!' Probably one of the most graphic 'Ahas' I ever had in my life was when I was reading Viktor Frankl's **'Man's Search for Meaning'**. He was describing all kinds of horrors that we needn't go into here. In the midst of all this killing, death, and torment, he came to the realisation and awareness of the greatest pearl of wisdom, in my opinion, yet uttered by a human being. This pearl is so powerful that I'll not hold back and disguise it or dilute it in any way. This truth simply states that:

THE A - Z OF POSITIVE THINKING

> *'The ultimate freedom, the final freedom we all have, that can never be taken away from us, is the ability to choose our attitude in any set of circumstances'.*

Frankl saw individuals dividing into two types. There are those that give up hope: 'Woe is me, poor me. Why has this terrible thing happened to me? There is nothing I can do to help myself.' Others say to themselves: 'OK. I can accept this. I accept that this is awful, that I don't particularly enjoy this happening to me. But what can I do to improve the matter? I'm going to get out of this jam. I'm going to do everything humanly possible to make the best of this situation by looking at what I can do personally. What is within my own power to influence, perhaps to change and rectify this situation?'

I imagine that if you're like me (human) you've probably come across examples of these attitudes either in your own experience or seen them in friends, relatives, colleagues, and peers. There are those who acquiesce, abdicate, and stop growing. And there are those who decide to take personal responsibility for their own thoughts and circumstances.

To show that there is nothing new in the world of ideas, when it comes to people's attitudes and behaviour, I'd like to draw on some wisdom from 2,500 years ago, from classical Greece. The scholar and philosopher Plato had many adages but the one that holds unbelievable currency today is that he believed, like Frankl, that people gravitate towards two zones, a zone of influence and a zone of concern. (See Figure1.)

THE A - Z OF POSITIVE THINKING

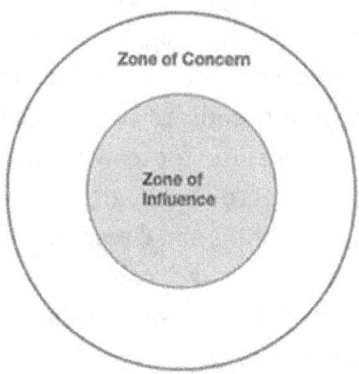

FIGURE 1
Zones of Influence and Concern

Now people who operate totally in their zone of concern are generally people who are out of control, who are continually moaning about this, that, or the other. We've all met them. You know the conversations...

'Oh, why won't the government do…', 'If only the company would…', 'Typical, isn't it? Just look at the weather! Why it always does this I don't know.' You catch the message?

You see, people who operate away from their zone of influence are caught in the habit of looking continually outside of themselves for solutions. They adopt an external habit and want others to make everything right with their world. Does that make sense? Of course, it doesn't! It's not looking for solutions that are within their control.

So, let's look at the other zone, the zone of influence, and see what a difference it makes. There always seem to be crises going on in the world. Famines, wars, ethnic cleansing, despots, terrorism…

THE A - Z OF POSITIVE THINKING

Now individually we probably have the attitude that there is not a heck of a lot we can do about any of them, outside of donating or perhaps even lobbying. We may be concerned but we probably do not have much influence at this precise point in time, right?

People who are what is termed 'well-centred' will recognise this. They may well be concerned, but say, 'Let's focus on what we can do to influence', or even more importantly, 'Let's grow ourselves, our zone, to start having an influence on those areas that we are concerned with.' For instance, I know a man who works for the Crown Agents. He was vitally concerned about the issues in Bosnia and so created a position for himself whereby he could have an influence, using all his skills in people management and logistics to make a difference.

He ensured that the aid convoys got through to where they were needed. He grew his zone of influence to encompass part of his zone of concern.

That, in essence, is what a positive attitude is about: the ability to choose the attitude we want in a given set of circumstances and then to go out and do something about it. It doesn't have to be so graphic and serious. It could just be something simple, like something that happened to me, where an old school friend called up and said,

'We have not talked or seen each other in a while, and so I thought I'd do something about it.' Is that a positive, proactive action and attitude or what?

So pick up that phone, write that letter, tell your partner how much you love them and what they mean to you, but more importantly, do it now. Be influential in your own world

THE A - Z OF POSITIVE THINKING

Life is BETTER —WITH— Friends

THOUGHTS

Another pearl of wisdom that sometimes helps to clarify which zone we are in is the well-known quote from Reinhold Niebuhr:

'Grant me the serenity to accept the things that I cannot change, the courage to change those that I can, and the wisdom to know the difference'.

The difference between those situations that you cannot change and those that you can change, the difference between our zone of concern and our zone of influence is only our attitude, and our attitude is dictated by our thoughts alone.

Let me give you a personal example. I was sitting down with Caroline, a friend of mine, a while back, having a great conversation and a coffee, when she said, 'NJ, do you really

THE **A - Z** OF POSITIVE THINKING

believe all this stuff you talk about, that no matter what happens, you can control your thoughts and that this will make it all right?'

I said I did and gave her this example. 'I'm in this relationship with a wonderful woman, someone I think the world of, when at 8 p.m. one evening the phone rings. Now at 7:59 p.m. these are my exact thoughts and feelings about her:

Hope, Love, Future, Joy, Togetherness, Adventure, Sensuality, Growth, Ecstasy, Friendship, Kindred Spirits, Closeness, Intimacy, Happiness, Respect, Delight, Faith, Warmth, Honesty, Desire, Power, Trust.

Thoughts that she's very special. A clear picture, right? 'Now, at precisely 8 p.m., just a few seconds after all these strong positive feelings and thoughts, as a consequence of one thing she said to me on the phone, my thoughts are:

Gutted, Sick, Cold, Angry, Disappointed, Disbelieving, Disempowered, Hurt, Discarded, Jealous, Lost, Sad, Very Sad, Betrayal, Fearful, Tearful, Poor-Me, Why-Me, Pessimistic, Bereft...

A very different picture, agreed?

'But what had really changed, what had happened here? At one moment I was feeling on top of the world, positive and strong; at the next I'm feeling destroyed. Nothing physical had occurred, but mentally I had taken a message (and it could have been any message), internalised it and instantly, because of my attitude, I had changed my whole mentality.

THE **A - Z** OF POSITIVE THINKING

My whole attitude shifted from a positive frame to a negative one. I had changed myself in the way I'd reacted to the news.

'Now, did I stay there? Of course not, because I know the value of looking at my thoughts and my zones of influence. I know that in any given set of circumstances I have the freedom to choose my attitude. I would like to say that I'd reversed the whole scenario just as quickly, but I'm still learning and growing too.

By 8:30 p.m. though, I had begun to grasp the elemental truths of what I needed to do.

I began to think to myself, wait a minute here, let's look at this situation, if this is how I was feeling (**Hope, Love, Joy, Friendship...) and this is how I'm feeling now (Angry, Hurt, Lost, Tearful...**), which do I prefer? Well, there was no contest.

The 7:59 list definitely made me feel more empowered.

'So, I made the conscious decision to start to switch back to the positives because, let's be honest, what had really changed? I had been presented with a situation that was out of my immediate zone of influence. Somebody else (irrespective of how much I might love them) had made a decision that, for them, at that precise moment in time, was right and important. The opportunity I had been presented with was to look at my own attitude, take responsibility for controlling my own thoughts and think: Serenity, Courage and Wisdom.

'Sure, I could have gone out and got blind drunk, like I always had in the past when confronted with such emotional issues – but I didn't.

THE **A - Z** OF POSITIVE THINKING

Sure, I could have stayed angry, bitter, feeling sorry for myself, and built up a portfolio of hate, jealousy, why-me? And all that negative baggage – but I didn't. How constructive would those coping strategies have been? Instead, I took control.

'I decided to see this situation as an opportunity to focus on the positives, on how I still really was feeling beneath all this anger. I used the thought antidotes continually to stay in a positive frame of mind. I listened to that still quiet voice deep within and I looked for a way forward.

'The results were quite dramatic. My whole demeanour changed very rapidly. I became very aware that I was in control. A few days later when we met, we had the most constructive, positive, loving time together we'd ever had. So yes, Caroline, I do believe that no matter what happens, we can control our thoughts.'

So, when somebody decides to pull our chain, when something unexpected occurs that knocks us away from our centre, let's look back to that centre, take charge and choose in Frankl's words, 'the attitude we want in any given situation'.

Let's acknowledge our ultimate freedom: the freedom to choose and make the circumstances that we desire.

THE **A - Z** OF POSITIVE THINKING

POSITIVE THINKING

THE ANTIDOTES: HOW TO USE THEM

Albert Schweitzer said:
> *'People must cease attributing their problems to their environment and again learn to exercise their will, their personal responsibility.'*

What are the antidotes? How do they help you to stay positive? They are an exercise in taking responsibility for what goes into our minds. They are a living list of words. They are positive, strong, vital words, words that evoke feelings of strength and control, words that raise positive emotions, words to aspire to, to move towards and words to whisper to our loved ones.

THE **A - Z** OF POSITIVE THINKING

They may be words that you feel apply to you or another. Perhaps if you're in love or in a relationship you may want to go through the list and highlight the ones that you feel are applicable to your lover. Remember though that when you do:

'What we see in others is invariably what we see within ourselves.'

So you cannot fail to give yourself a boost too. It's the ultimate win-win of a present: not only do you give but you also receive.

Another way of using the words is to dip in whenever a negative event, comment or thought comes winging its way towards you, like I just did a moment ago, when I realised there was a nagging doubt eating away at the edges of my consciousness.

It has been shown that it is impossible to hold two contrary thoughts in our mind at the sametime. I can guarantee that if you've got a negative one and you look down through the antidotes, picking out the ones that speak to you, that negative thought will not stick around for long. It will very quickly ride out of town.

Another way of using them is to use what are known as 'present-tense sentence stems', attaching the antidotes. For example:

> **I am Happy, I am Trusting,
> I am Spectacular.
> I am Brilliant, I am Free,
> I am Phenomenal… or
> I have a Mentor,
> I have Love,
> I have Health.
> I have a Bright Future;
> I have Good Friends…**

THE **A - Z** OF POSITIVE THINKING

The stems are a way of acknowledging who we are and what we really have going for us in our lives.

Can you see that the antidotes then become completely personal to you and you alone? They can be used for positive affirmations, personal mottoes, goal setting, vision and mission. Best of all, they are constantly and forever renewable; they are not a limited resource, something that can be taken away. Rest assured you cannot run out of them, and they are always there for you. Your imagination is the only limitation.

So, let's turn to these mysterious and positive words and let's go explore, looking for the words that may change your life or at the very least some of your perceptions.

Happy Antidoting and remember, you cannot overdose on positive thoughts.

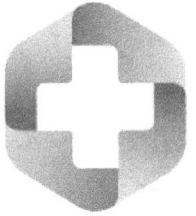

THE JAMES PHARMACY INSTRUCTIONS

PLEASE READ CAREFULLY

Remember, antidotes are for poisons and negative thoughts are the poisons of the mind. If you do not have the poison, you do not need the antidote. If you do, then take several hundred of them every day from the moment you awake to the instant you sleep.

THE **A - Z** OF POSITIVE THINKING

You may find some side effects that catch you unawares. One common consequence is that you may find yourself smiling and laughing uncontrollably at the strange negative antics of those around you who are not on the same medication, who are not antidoting. Do not be discouraged. You are sane.

These positive word capsules are very, very good for you. Keep taking the tablets.

THE ANTIDOTES

THE ANTIDOTES

Ambitious, Amazing, Adventurous, Achiever, Ahead, Alive, Alert, Alluring, Adonis, Allowed, Allah, Amiable, Amicable, Amorous, Amused, Adored, Adroit, Anointed, Ardent, Artistic, Assertive, Astral, Atman, Attractive, Authentic, Able, Absorbed, Antidotal, Apollo, Awesome, Apostolic, Action, Ace, Acclaimed, Accomplished, Adonai, Alpha and Omega, Assured, Achieve, Active, Adept, Admired, Aphrodite, Aesthetic, Aspiring, Attitude, Animated, Agile, Angel, Ability, Ablaze, Athletic, Ascending, Arriviste

THE ANTIDOTES

Bouncy, Blissful, Brilliant, Beautiful, Balanced, Bearing, Beatific, Believe, Beloved, Begin, Beneficent, Benefactor, Benign, Benevolent, Be, Buddha, Blatant, Broadminded, Bewitch, Blessed, Bold, Bonny, Boss, Bountiful, Brainy, Bacchus, Boyish, Brave, Brazen, Breathe, Butterfly, Brahma, Bright, Ballistic, Ballsy, Boost, Born, Bouncing, Balm

THE ANTIDOTES

Centred, Creative, Colourful, Committed, Calm, Can, Candid, Champion, Change, Celebrate, Cerebral, Certain, Character, Cheeky, Caesar, Curious, Confident, Conscious, Control, Cool, Cosmopolitan, Cracker, Crazy, Cultivated, Compassionate, Competent, Composed, Conquering, Considerate, Constant, Constructive, Contemplative, Content, Classic, Czar, Christ, Clever, Cognisant, Comical, Commanding, Communicator, Courageous, Carpe diem, Clear, Capable, Capacity, Captivating, Care, Catholic, Chief, Chivalrous, Chuckle,

THE ANTIDOTES

Creating, Commitment, Cleave, Cherish, Charged, Charity, Charm, Cock-a-hoop, Confucian, Caress, Cathartic, Certitude, Captivate, Composed, Congratulations, Cohere, Coherent, Coach, Conviviality, Creativity, Congruity, Congenial, Congruous, Charisma, Charismatic, Celestial, Caring, Contrary

THE ANTIDOTES

Deserving, Dynamic, Dancing, Desired, Deserve, Diagnose, Direct, Discover, Doctor, Draw, Duplicate, Deduce, Defend, Deliver, Demand, Deny, Differ, Diligent, Dominate, Delighted, Destined, Distinguished, Diamond, Dance, Dapper, Dashing, Delight, Decide, Dedicate, Decisive, Determined, Disciplined, Drive, Direction, Desire, Dream, Dripple, Develop, Diversity, Diverse, Developing, Dalliance, Delicious, Design, Descant, Doughty, Dreamy, Devoted, Devotion

THE ANTIDOTES

Energetic, Exciting, Enthusiastic, Extraordinary, Envisage, Equilibrate, Enfranchise, Equitable, Erotic, Escape, Efficacious, Effuse, Educe, Effect, Evolve, Ecstatic, Eclectic, Excited, Elegant, Elevate, Elucidate, Embody, Enable, Enamour, Enchant, Entice, Essential, Ethereal, Endow, Enhance, Enigma, Enormous, Ensure, Entertain, Enthral, Enthralling, Expect, Endure, Exotic, Extroverted, Enterprising, Eagle, Earnest, Easy-going, Eccentric, Entrance, Esteem, Exercise, Eager, Educate, Encourage, Experience, Excel, Enlighten, Empower, Equal, Ebullient, Evolving, Encouragement, Education, Equality, Embrace, Everlasting

THE ANTIDOTES

Fun, Free, Friends, Fame, Funny, Father, Female, Fabulous, Facilitator, Facet, Face, Fair, Faithful, Famous, Fancy, Fantastic, Featured, Fascinating, Fashionable, Fast, Favoured, Favourite, Fearless, Feasible, Felicitous, Felicity, Focused, Faith, Find, Feel, Found, Fortunate, Fiery, Foxy, Fellowship, Feminine, Forerunner, Foresee, Foresight, Forgive, Form, Formative, Formidable, Forthright, Fortify, Fortitude, Fortuitous, Fortune, **Feeling, Flourishing, Forgiving, Freeing,** Fortunate, Forward, Founder, Foster, Fountain, Fragrant, Frank,

THE ANTIDOTES

Fraternal, Freelance, Freedom, Fresh, Friendly, Frugal, Fruitful, Fertile, Fervent, Festive, Fidelity, Fighter, Figurative, Finalist, Financial, Finder, Fine, Finesse, Finisher, Firm, First, Fisherman, Flamboyant, Flora, Fulfilled, Fulfilment, Fundamental, Future, Fit, Fitting, Flair, Flattered, Flavour, Flexible, Fluent, Fluid, Flying, Focused, Forcible, Forceful, Foremost, Founding, Flow, Flowing, Fulgent, Fiancée, Friendship

THE ANTIDOTES

Growing, Glowing, Giving, Glittering, Great, Good, Gallant, Golden, Grandiose, Guide Guiding, Green, Guru, Galactic, Gambler, Gatherer, Gay, Gaiety, Genuine, Giant, Gigantic, Giggle, Gladiator, Glamorous, Graphic, Gleeful, Gnostic, Go-ahead, Godly, Glad, Golden-Rule, Goluptious, Good Looking, Goodwill, Goodly, Governor, Graced, Gracious, Graduate, Grafter, Grand, Grateful, Gregarious, Gorgeous, Generous, God, Glorious, Genius, Genteel, Gentle, Gumption, Gala

THE ANTIDOTES

Happy, Healthy, Horny, Holy, Handsome, Handy, Hardy, Headstrong, Ha-ha, Harmonious, Hearty, Healing, Heart, Heaven, Heed, Hegemony, Hegemonic, Helmsman, Helpful, Herald, Heroic, Herself, Heterodox, Hewer, High, High-spirited, High-flyer, Hermes, Hindu, Honest, Hustle, Halcyon, Hale, High-minded, Hilarious, Himself, Hip, Historic, Hit, Homeric, Honey, Honeyed, Honoured, Honourable, Hoot, Hopeful, Hospitable, Host, Huge, Humming, Human, Humane, Humanist, Humble, Humility, Humour, Humorous, Hunter, Hustle, Hygienic, Hearten, Harmony, Holistic

THE ANTIDOTES

Inspiring, Intimate, Inquisitive, Irresistible, Improviser, Impulsive, Increasing, Illuminated, Illustrator, Illustrious, Imaginative, Immanent, Immanence, Immanuel, Impassioned, Impelled, Impressive, Impromptu, Improving, Insightful, Isis, Insistent, Instigator, Instructive, Instrumental, Intellectual, Intelligent, Intense, Intending, Invulnerable, Independent, Individual, Industrious, Infatuated, Infinite, Inflamed, Influential, Informed, Ingenious, Initiator, Innate, Innocent, Inquiring, Interesting, International, Interpretive, Intrepid, Intrigued, Invaluable,

THE ANTIDOTES

Inventive, Investigator, Invigorating, Invincible, Inviting, Impart, Impartial, Interdependent, Impeccable, Imperative, Imperial, Impish, Imposing, Impossible, Indescribable, Indomitable, Independent, Immune, Imminent, Immense, Inspired, Inspirational, Initiative, Iconoclast, Idealist, Igneous, Imbued, Immaculate, Irrepressible, Immediate, Insatiable, Integrate, Integration, Integral

THE ANTIDOTES

Jubilant, Joyful, Jammy, Juicy, Je Ne Sais Quoi, Jewel, Just, Jah, Jasmine, Jaunt, Jaunty, Jest, Jesting, Jester, Jewel, Jinks, Jocular, Jocund, Joke, Joking, Jesus, Jolly, Jollification, Jovial, Jubilance, Jubilation, Jubilee, Judicious, Jehovah, Joyous, Joy

Knowing, Keen, Kissing, Kind, Knack, Kudos, Knowledgeable, Karma, Kindly, Kindle, King, Kindred, Knight, Kaleidoscopic, Keeper, Krishna, Key, Kiss

THE ANTIDOTES

Living, Laughing, Loving, Learning, Laudable, Laureate, Leader, Lean, Legend, Lucid, Luminous, Lord, Levity, Luminary, Leitmotif, Liberal, License, Life, Lifespring, Liked, Lion, Lissom, Loquacious, Lucky, Luscious, Liberty, Lateral, Lavish, Locus, Lode, Lofty, Logical, Logos, Long-lived, Lyrical, Luxuriant, Love, Light, Lusty, Listen, Lively, Laconic, Lantern, Light, Lascivious, Latent, Light-headed, Libra, Light-hearted, Light-minded, Like-minded, Lifelong, Lift, Lifeblood, Lyrical, Lucid, Luminous, Lusty

THE ANTIDOTES

Motivated, Magical, Marvellous, Myself, Mastery, Mutual, Motion, Momentum, Mindful, Minded, Miracle, Miraculous, Mirror, Mirth, Mission, Mitigate, Mnemonic, Mobile, Moderate, Modern, Modest, Modifier, Momentous, Moral, More, Mother, Most, Male, Motor, Mountainous, Mover, Mystery, Mysterious, Mystical, Mythic, Mana, Manitou, Munificent, Muse, Music, Mutual, Memorable, Mentor, Merciful, Meritorious, Machiavellian, Maestro, Magic, Magisterial, Magnetic, Magnificent, Main, Majestic, Merry, Mesmeric, Messenger,

THE ANTIDOTES

Multifaceted, Maker, Manful, Managerial, Manic, Mannered, Marvel, Massive, Master, Mature, Mercy, Maximalist, Mediate, Mediator, Mellow, Melodic, Metamorphosis, Mahatma, Mecca, Meteoric, Motivated, Move, Meaning, Manage, **Masterful,** Model, Magnanimous, Methodical, Meticulous, Mohammed, Mien, Might, Millionaire, Madonna

THE ANTIDOTES

Natural, Novel, Nobel, Now, Necessary, Neat, Navigator, Negotiate, Neophyte, Nerve, Nice, Nirvana, Noisy, Nonconformist, Notable, Nourish, Nourishing, Nurture, Nubile, Numen, Numinousness, Nature, Nectar, Nestle, Nimble, Nymph, Notice, Notional, Numerate

THE ANTIDOTES

Original, Optimistic, Open-minded, Oneness, Objective, Obliging, Observing, Observant, Odyssey, Oedipus, Olympian, Omnipotent, Omniscient, Orgasm, Opportune, Opportunity, Optimist, Optimism, Options, Opulent, Oracle, Orator, Ordained, Ordered, Organised, Osmotic, Outlandish, Outlook, Outspoken, Overt, Ownership, Opportunist, Obstinate, Organic, Orgasmic

THE ANTIDOTES

Positive, Powerful, Persistent, Passionate, Prominent, Providence, Perfect, Performer, Permanent, Pace, Pacific, Paean, Pagan, Painter, Palatable, Panache, Par, Paragon, Paramount, Pantheism, Pan, Pardon, Par Excellence, Parity, Partake, Part, Participate, Participant, Partner, **Peaceful, Precious, Playful, Phenomenal,** Patient, Peace, Peak, Pearl, Penetrate, Pensive, Perceived, Perceptive, Perennial, Permeate, Permit, Perpetual, Persevere, Persist, Persistent, Person, Personable, Personify, Perspective, Perspicacious,

THE ANTIDOTES

Perspicuous, Penetrating, Persuade, Persuasive, Pertinent, Pervasive, Pharos, Phenomenon, Philander, Philanthropist, Philosopher, Philosophical, Phlegmatic, Phoenix, Photographic, Photogenic, Physical, Pillar, Pilot, Pioneer, Pious, Piquant, Placate, Platonic, Plausible, Play, Please, Pleasure, Pleasurable, Plenitude, Plucky, Plus, Poignant, Point, Pointed, Poised, Polemic, Polished, Polite, Pomp, Ponder, Popular, Positive, Positivist, Possess, Possible, Possibility, Postulate, Potent, Potential, Pounce, Practice, Practical, Pragmatic, Praise,

THE ANTIDOTES

Pray, Precognition, Preconceive, Predispose, Precede, Predisposition, Prefigure, Premeditation, Premonition, Prepossess, Presuppose, Polymath, Privileged, **Precious, Progressive, Professional, Profound,** Precedence, Precedent, Precipitate, Precise, Proud, Precocious, Precursor, Predecessor, Predict, Premeditate, Predominate, Prefer, Preference, Preferential, Premier, Pride, Prepared, Prescient, Present, Presence, Presentable, Preside, Press, Prestige, Presume, Prestigious, Presumption, Presumptive, Pretty, Prevail, Prevalent,

— THE ANTIDOTES

Primacy, Prime, Principal, Pristine, Private, Privy, Prized, Proceed, Process, Procure, Prod, Prodigy, Produce, Productive, Profess, Proficient, Profit, Progress, Project, Projection, Prominent, Promise, Promote, Prompt, Propensity, Prophet, Propitious, Propose, Prospect, Prosper, Protect, Protest, Prove, Provide, Prowess, Prudent, Psychic, Punctual, Pupil, Pure, Purity, Purify, Purpose, Pursuant, Push, Perfection, Providential

THE ANTIDOTES

Quick, Quiet, Questing, Quoted, Qualify, Quality, Query, Question, Quicken, Quaker, Quiet, Quiescent, Quintessence, Quintessential, Quixotic, Quizzical

THE ANTIDOTES

Radiant, Relaxed, Romantic, Rich, Resourceful, Responsible, Resolute, Respected, Reveal, Recognise, Relax, Relaxing, Raconteur, Racy, Radiance, Radiate, Radical, Rally, Randy, Rabbi, Revered, Rapt, Rapturous, Rate, Rational, Rationalise, Ray, Reconstruct, Readdress, Reaffirm, Rearrange, Reassert, Reassess, Refund, Rebuild, Recharge, Recommence, Reconsider, Redress, Recover, Recreate, Redirect, Razzle, Rediscover, Redistribute, Re-embark, Re-emerge, Reinforce, Relive, Re-establish, Refashion, Reform, Refuse, Reinvigorate, Remake, Remodel, Rigorous,

THE ANTIDOTES

Reorganise, Revalue, Reach, Real, Realise, Reap, Reason, Reasonable, Reassure, Reassured, Rebound, Recall, Reciprocate, Receive, Rejoicing, Resurgent, Ready, Rare, Recognise, Recollect, Recommend, Recommended, Reconcile, Recuperate, Recusant, Redouble, Redress, Refine, Refined, Reflective, Reformer, Refresh, Regal, Regard, Reinforce, Rejoice, Relate, Relativist, Released, Relevant, Relief, Relieve, Relinquished, Relinquish, Relish, Remarkable, Remembered, Reminiscent, Renaissance, Renewed, Renowned, Repaired, Repeat, Replenished, Reputable,

THE ANTIDOTES

Requested, Required, Rescued, Reservoir, Resilient, Resistance, Resolute, Resolved, Resonant, Resourceful, Respected, Respectable, Resplendent, Responsive, Responsible, Responsibility, Rested, Restful, Restorative, Restrained, Restraint, Results, Resurrected, Retentive, Retrieved, Retrospective, Revelation, Revered, Reverence, Revolutionary, Rhapsodical, Rhetorical, Rhythm, Rhythmic, Right, Righteous, Rising, Robust, Romanticist, Rosy, Rounded, Rover, Royal, Rubicon, Rugged, Running, Rushing

THE ANTIDOTES

Singing, Smiling, Sparkling, Supporting, Stylish, Splendid, Sensual, Searching, Smile, Sincere, Slim, Self-help, Strong, Sacred, Sacrifice, Sacrosanct, Safe, Sagacious, Sage, Sailing, Saint, Saintly, Salient, Sally, Salubrious, Salutary, Salvation, Sanctify, Sanctuary, Sane, Spring, Seductive, Sanguine, Sartorial, Sanguineous, Satisfied, Saucy, Saturn, Sangfroid, Savoirfaire, Savoirvivre, Scholar, Scholarly, Scholastic, Scientific, Scrumptious, Scrupulous, Sculpturesque, Searcher, Searching, Secluded, Secular, Secure, Sedate, Surprising, Sympathetic,

THE ANTIDOTES

Seductive, Sedulous, See, Seeing, Seen, Selective, Self-control, Self-confident, Self-determined, Self-educated, Self-esteem, Self-realisation, Self-respect, Self-starter, Self-will, Self-willed, Sense, Sensible, Sensitive, Sensuous, Sentiment, Sentimental, Separate, Serene, Serious, Serve, Share, Sharing, Sharp, Shimmer, Shine, Shiny, Shipshape, Showman, Significant, Significance, Sikh, Silent, Silence, Simmering, Simple, **Sunny, Serene, Successful, Someone,** Singular, Skilful, Skilled, Sleek, Slender, Slick, Smashing, Smile, Smooth, Smoulder, Sociable, Social,

THE ANTIDOTES

Socratic, Solace, Solutions, Solve, Somebody, Sonorous, Sophisticated, Sorry, Soul, Space, Spark, Speak, Special, Specific, Spectacle, Speculate, Speedy, Spellbinder, Spellbound, Spirit, Soul-mate, Spiritual, Splendid, Splendour, Spontaneous, Spring, Stable, Stand-up, Star, Start, Stature, Status, Steadfast, Steady, Steersman, Sterling, Still, Stimulating, Stoic, Stout, Straight, Strategist, Strength, Strenuous, Stretch, Stress, Stringent, Strong, Struggle, Study, Studious, Stupendous, Sturdy, Style, Stylish, Subdue, Sublime, Substance, Substantial, Subtle, Succeed,

THE ANTIDOTES

Success, Succinct, Succour, Succulent, Sufficient, Suffuse, Suggest, Suitable, Sumptuous, Super, Superb, Superfine, Superhuman, Superintend, Superior, Superlative, Superman, Supernatural, Supervise, Supple, Support, Striking, **Spectacular, Sensational, Sensual,** Sunny, Supportive, Supreme, Sure, Sunshine, Surprise, Survive, Survey, Sustain, Sweet, Sweetheart, Sweetie, Swell, Swift, Swim, Swing, Swot, Sylph, Siva, Sympathy, Synchronise, Synoptic, Synthesise, Systematic, Synergy, Synthesis, Sexy

THE ANTIDOTES

Talented, Tasty, Terrific, Trusting, Tasteful, Tempestuous, Tempting, Tender, Tacit, Taciturn, Tact, Tactical, Tactile, Taking-off, Talkative, Tall, Tally, Tangible, Target, Targeted, Taste, Teach, Teacher, Teamster, Technical, Technique, Teem, Teetotal, Teleological, Temperate, Tempestuous, Tenacious, Tenacity, Theatrical, Therapeutic, Thin, Thinking, Thinker, Thorough, Thoughtful, Thread, Threshold, Thrilled, Thrusting, Ticking, Tidy, Timeless, Timely, Tireless, Titillator, Titillating, Toast, Together, Tolerant, Tops, Topical, Torrid, Total, Touching, Tough,

THE ANTIDOTES

Toward, Tower, Track, Traditional, Trainer, Tranquil, Transcend, Transcendental, Transfigured, Transformed, Transit, Transition, Translator, Transmit, Transpire, Transpiration, Transported, **Thrilling, Thankful, Treasured, True,** Travail, Travel, Traveller, Treasure, Treat, Tremendous, Triad, Tribute, Trim, Triumph, Triumphant, True-Love, Truism, Truly, Trust, Truth, Truthful, Try, Trying, Tuition, Tune, Turning-point, Tutor, Tutelage, Twinkle, Tumultuous, Tickle, Tickling

THE ANTIDOTES

Undeniable, Unequalled, Useful, Unique, Utopia, Utopian, Unquenchable, Unrivalled, Unpredicted, Unprecedented, Unmatched, Unerring, Unearthly, Unpressured, Unity. Unperturbed, Unpretentious, Unrestrained, Upright, Urgent, Unorthodox, Upshot, Unity

THE ANTIDOTES

Vivacious, **Vigilant, Vivid, Virile**, Vigorous, Venus, Valiant, Valuable, Vegetarian, Verbal, Veritable, Vibrate, Victor, Victory, Victorious, Vishnu, Virtuous, Vocal, Vogue, Volatile, Voyager, Visualise, Values, Vibrant, Vital, Vitality

Wonderful, **Warm, Wealthy, Wild,** Well, Worthy, Wise, Wakeful, Watchful, Wanton, Weird, Wholesome, Wide, Wicked, Woo, Work, Worldly, Worship, Worthwhile, Whole, Wilful, Willing, Winner, Winning, Witty, Within-Without, Wondrous

THE ANTIDOTES

eXcelling, eXciting, eXpecting, eXploring, eXtraordinary, eXtravagant, eXuberant, eXultant, eXtrovert, eXtra, eXtra Special, eXperiment, eXperimental, eXplain, eXplore, eXpress, eXpressive, eXquisite, eXternalise, eXtol, eXcellent, eXcite, eXcuse others, eXercise, eXert, eXhort, eXpect, eXpedite, eXperience, eXpectation

— THE ANTIDOTES

Young, Yearning, Yours, Yes,
Youthful, Yahweh, Yes to Life

Zippy, Zealous, Zestful, Zeus,
Zeitgeist, Zonal, Zoroastrian

THE A - Z OF POSITIVE THINKING
SO WHY BOTHER?

I'd imagine that, like many people I've talked to as a consequence of their reading of this book, in places you've smiled and in places you've frowned. Some of it's for you and some of it's not. That's OK by me, because it's the smiles I'm looking for and anything that can be done to reverse that statistic of three times the negativity is pretty wonderful stuff.

The question was asked though, why bother? That's a good question on many different fronts. James Allen in his essay 'As a Man Thinketh' says:

> *'It is not what we want but what we are'*
> *and 'A man is literally what he thinks,*
> *his character being the complete sum of*
> *all his thoughts.'*

Marcus Aurelius wrote:
> *'We become as our thoughts are usually and habitually.'*

I've included a quote already:
> *'The important issue is not so much what we think we want, but more a case of what we want to think.'*

The core theme is that without control over our thoughts, what chance is there for our dreams? And that's a vitally important issue to bother with, wouldn't you say?

Let's analyse the above quote, 'It's not so much what we think we want.' Let's ask ourselves the question, what is it that we think we want? Ask it again and again, write down the answers. Then ask the question, what thoughts do we have associated with these wants?

THE A - Z OF POSITIVE THINKING

Quite often what I find in working with individuals and groups is that the thoughts that they are having are incongruous with what they want.

For example, somebody thinks to themselves that they want peace, affiliation, career, wealth, friendship, success, acknowledgement, intimacy etc. Yet the actual thoughts they associate with these wants are things like anger, frustration, unworthiness, fright, fear, anxiety, reluctance to give up status quo or perceived stability. It becomes apparent why the actual road towards those wants is slow going, if at all feasible.

No, it's the second part of the quote that has the real payback, *'It's a case of what we want to think, that's important.'* Try it. Look again at the things that you think you want and now think of the thoughts that would be essential and congruous in allowing those things to happen.

What thoughts are necessary to put you back on the path to your dreams? I'd be willing to bet a million that they need to be positive, not negative.

Now we realise that we have to control them continuously to stay in harmony with everything we want from life.

To get everything good and beautiful out of life we have to know what we want to think. This truism cannot be emphasised enough. We are literally the sum total of our thoughts. The last freedom that we have is the ability to choose the attitude we want in any given circumstances. The people who get on in this world are the people who go out and look for the circumstances they want and if they can't find them, they make them. Well-centred people realise that they have to stay where they can make a difference, instead of having 'Pity-Parties' about things outside their zone, about concerns they have no influence over.

THE A - Z OF POSITIVE THINKING

We are our thoughts, and that realisation is a challenging issue for some people to accept. It can also be a courageous, serene, and wise decision to accept it. Indeed, acceptance is a positive step, and positive steps are associated with positive thoughts. You have here 1,705 helpful positive steps.

THE FREEDOM PROCESS

Socrates' famous dictum, 'First Know Thyself' is as relevant today as ever. On the following pages, Freedom is used as a step-by-step framework in helping us to find our own unique, independent, and individual purposes. It is a process of finding what we want from life and a useful, positive first step on the path to truly knowing ourselves.

Freedom occurs when many interrelated events happen simultaneously. By working on different areas of someone's life, a certain synergy commences which helps move them along their path. It is a continuous and creative endeavour.

The best way to use the action points is to look at each principle as a stepping-stone question. What do I want to focus on? What fears are hindering me right now?

THE **A - Z** OF POSITIVE THINKING

Where do I need to take responsibility? How can I gain more energy? What am I enthusiastic about? What disciplines would empower me?

Note that this is just a first step, but as the ancient sage Lao Tzu said,

> *'Even a thousand-mile journey starts with a single step.'*

Make masses of notes. Be positive. Start your journey now.

FREEDOM

'No person is truly free, who is not Master of themselves'

EPICTETUS

Step 1: Fearlessness and Focus

Do you allow the fear of change and a lack of direction to dissipate your focus? Personal freedom comes from discovering your real purpose.

- What do I need to Focus on right now?
- Stay in the present moment. Focus on what you want to think.
- What Feelings and Fears do I need to face up to?

THE A - Z OF POSITIVE THINKING
fReedom

'People must cease attributing their problems to their environment and again learn to exercise their will, their own personal responsibility'

ALBERT SCHWEITZER

Step 2: Roles and Responsibility

How do you respond to choices? Do you procrastinate or seize the moment? Are you aware that your relationship with yourself is your responsibility alone?

- Where do I need to take Responsibility?

- What do I want to see happen in my Relationships?

- Reach Decisions about what you are going to do. What is your Role to be?

frEedom

'The greatest discovery of my generation is that human beings can alter their lives by altering their attitudes of mind'

WILLIAM JAMES

Step 3: Esteem and Experience

How much faith do you truly have in yourself and your abilities? Do you visualise success to develop even more confidence? Do you nurture a sense of self-efficacy?

- When was the last time you Exercised your mind?

- Do you examine your Experiences and notice where your Self-Esteem comes from?

- Enlightenment will come with all those Ahas. Write them all down.

THE **A - Z** OF POSITIVE THINKING

fre**E**dom

'Our bodies are our gardens, Our wills are the gardeners'

WILLIAM SHAKESPEARE

Step 4: Energy and Enthusiasm

Have you ever assessed the cost that negative thoughts and people can have?

Discover the control you can develop with an attitude that will sustain you.

- When did you last **E**xercise your body?

- Do you **E**ncourage **E**nthusiasm in all you do and with all the people you meet?

- **E**nergy makes the difference. (Find it. Harness it. Use it.)

FREE**D**OM

'Knowing what to do isn't enough unless you have the self-discipline to do it'

HARVEY McKAY

Step 5: **D**ecisions and **D**etachment

Do you get anxious and uncertain about making major decisions? Find the secret of relishing uncertainty and reduce your anxiety in times of stress.

- What **D**ecisions do I need to make?
- What **D**irections have I ever wanted to explore?
- **D**o you recognise that **D**etachment and **D**isassociation can lead to Freedom?
- What do I need to **D**etach from?

THE A - Z OF POSITIVE THINKING
FREEDOM

'Life is an opportunity. Take it'

CHINESE PROVERB

Step 6: Options and Opportunity

Have you ever rejected or not seen opportunities that were available? Look for the options that are there for you and that will allow you to rise above the negative attitudes of others.

- What **O**bstacles do I have to **O**ptimistically **O**vercome?

- Do I have an **O**pen-minded attitude to developing myself?

- How can **O**thers help me to learn and improve?

FREEDO**M**

'The greatest motivator of all is Love. Love what you do and Love who you are'

Step 7: **M**eaning and **M**otivation

Have you ever wondered why you do what you do, what the point of it all is? Learn to live with passion, inspiration, real commitment and sustainable *motivation*.

- Where does my **M**otivation come from?
- When do I have inner **M**otivation? Power comes from within.
- Do I recognise that being **M**yself is the most empowering strategy I can adopt?
- Have I realised that **M**astery comes from **M**oving ahead now, with **M**eaning?

THE A-Z OF POSITIVE THINKING

Nobody is perfect but your team can be
(www.perfectteams.co.uk)

The Freedom Process is just one of the frameworks available to our accredited associates and licensees [our advocates].

The one thing all our advocates have in common (besides being very positive) is they love the Perfect Teams product. They love the simplicity, clarity, and transparency.

The indicator, which is the first product most people experience, gives you a deeper understanding of your own individual character. It highlights the gifts you bring to the table. It shows you your blind spots.

TAKE THE TEST
[https://perfectteams.co.uk/account/login/register]

The team maps give you an instant team profile for your business. They help you to discover the make-up of your team, the characters you have, which ones are missing, and if you have the right people to take you forward.

PROFILE YOUR TEAM
[https://perfectteams.co.uk/account/login/register]

The workshop helps you to create awareness, cohesion, and unity. It resolves conflicts. Leading and running a business takes time and energy. Having a team that supports you takes away that pressure. Find your secret sauce.

BOOK A WORKSHOP
[https://www.perfectteams.co.uk/prices#books]

THE A - Z OF POSITIVE THINKING

> A consultation helps business owners to develop a vision. All organisations are a reflection of the leader.
> How far do you want to go?
>
> ENQUIRE HERE
> [https://www.perfectteams.co.uk/contact-us]

> The Perfect Teams Academy is the route to building your own practice using the Perfect Teams intellectual property (IP). If you want a deeper understanding and are looking for a 'Plug & Play' tool to help you build your own consultancy business.
>
> APPLY HERE
> https://jobso.id/d55p

BOOKS TO INSPIRE

- *As a Man Thinketh*, James Allen
- *Jonathan Livingstone Seagull*, Richard Bach
- *The Power of Myth*, Joseph Campbell
- *How to Win Friends and Influence People*, Dale Carnegie
- *Encyclopaedia Britannica*
- *Man's Search For Meaning*, Viktor Frankl
- *The Fear of Freedom*, Erich Fromm
- *The Common Denominator of Success*, Albert Grey
- *The Tao of Pooh*, Benjamin Hof
- *Think and Grow Rich*, Napoleon Hill
- *Get a Message to Garcia,* Elbert Hubberd
- *Search*, James Kavanaugh

THE A - Z OF POSITIVE THINKING

- *Will You Be My Friend*, James Kavanaugh
- *The Act of Creation*, Arthur Koestler
- *If you Meet the Buddha on the Road, Kill Him!*
- Sheldon Kopp
- *Effective Problem Solving*, Martin Levine
- *Managing Yourself*, Jagdish Parikh
- *The Road Less Traveled*, M. Scott Peck
- *The Man who Mistook his Wife for a Hat*, Oliver Sacks
- *The Alexander Technique*, Chris Stevens
- *The Way of Life*, Lao Tzu, trans. Witter Bynner
- *See You at the Top*, Zig Ziglar

If you liked the A to Z, you'll love the Freedom Tree
also by Neil Tuson

I've read a good number of personal development books, but this is certainly the most beautifully written and inspiring book I've ever read - **Howard**

I have finished reading your book and enjoyed it immensely - in fact I have put it on my son's bed for him to read to support him in a relationship dilemma he is experiencing now – **Ros**

I want to say that having read it, it is so inspirational, honest, real, touches the heart and is unput-downable – **Karen**

I love this book. It is so beautiful too – **Jenny**

THE **A - Z** OF POSITIVE THINKING

> If we always think
> what we have always thought,
> we will always be
> what we have always been.
>
> N James

www.ingramcontent.com/pod-product-compliance
Lightning Source LLC
Chambersburg PA
CBHW050258120526
44590CB00016B/2405